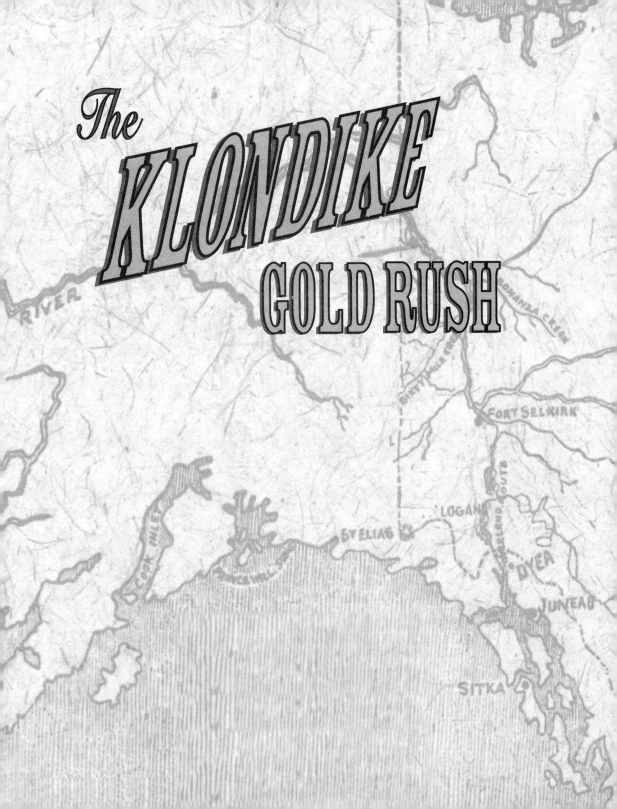

The KLONDIKE GOLD RUSH

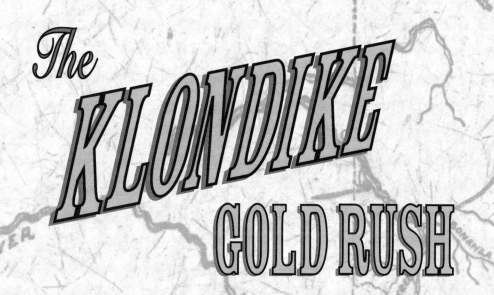

The KLONDIKE GOLD RUSH

Donna Walsh Shepherd

A FIRST BOOK

Franklin Watts

A DIVISION OF GROLIER PUBLISHING

NEW YORK   LONDON   HONG KONG   SYDNEY

DANBURY, CONNECTICUT

For John and Jessie Walsh and
Shannon and Spencer Walsh.
May your lives be rich with adventure

Thanks to the many who helped with this book, Sean O'Meara of the Seattle
headquarters of the Klondike Gold Rush Park, Steve Borell, executive director
of the Alaska Miners Association, and others.

Visit Franklin Watts on the Internet at:
http://publishing.grolier.com

Photographs ©: Alaska State Library: 45 (P.E. Larss Collection), 13; Alaska Stock Images: back cover, 24, 27, 28, 32, 35, 52 (Anchorage Museum), 9 (Chris Arend), 55 (Mark Kelley), 57 (Harry Walker); Culver Pictures: 20; Dawson City Museum: 15, 41, 51; James Marshall: 56; Museum of History & Industry: 18, 38, 49; North Wind Picture Archives: 46; Puget Sound Maritime Historical Society: 37; University of Washington Libraries: 21, 22, 26, 36, 40, 42 bottom, 44; UPI/Corbis-Bettmann: cover, 2, 30, 31, 34, 42 top, 43, 54.

Library of Congress Cataloging-in-Publication Data

Walsh Shepherd, Donna.
    The Klondike gold rush / by Donna Walsh Shepherd.
        p. cm. –(A First Book)
    Includes bibliographical references and index.
    Summary: Describes the adventures of those who flocked to the Klondike
after gold was discovered there in 1896.
        ISBN 0-531-20360-3 (lib. bdg.)   0-531-15909-4 (pbk.)
    1. Klondike River Valley (Yukon)—Gold discoveries—Juvenile literature.
[1. Klondike River Valley (Yukon)—Gold discoveries.] I. Title. II. Series.
F1095.K5W35   1998
971.9'19—dc21
                                                                   97–38340
                                                                      CIP
                                                                       AC

CONTENTS

A NOTE ABOUT MONEY

In the United States in 1898, $1 bought, on the average, what $48 will buy a hundred years later. The price of 1 ounce (28 grams) of gold in 1898 was $18, established by the government. Today the price of gold varies depending on what people will pay for it, usually from $350 to $400 an ounce. A ton of pure gold in 1898 was valued at about $672,000; today that gold is worth more than $13 million.

All dollar amounts given in this book are 1898 dollars, unless otherwise noted. When someone paid $1 for an egg or a banana, it was equivalent to paying $48 for a single egg or banana today. Paying $250 for a box of laundry starch in 1898 was like paying about $12,000 today. Prices were very high in the Klondike because there was so much gold, but little else. Goods were in high demand, and there was a lot of gold to pay for them. In today's dollars, it would cost from $12,000 to $24,000 for each miner to purchase the equipment he needed and make the journey north.

ONE

DEEP IN THE KLONDIKE GROUND

Since the days of our ancient ancestors, people have hungered for gold. The passion for this rare metal is born in the desire for wealth and power. This brilliant metal won't rust or corrode and is soft enough to work into shapes—sculptures to honor the gods, jewelry to decorate the rich, coins to buy whatever one might desire.

Clothes for powerful leaders have been made of gold—cloaks, sandals, gloves, and crowns. Gold can be hammered very thin and used for decorating our most precious books and documents. Today, we even use gold in dentistry and medicine to treat cancer and arthritis.

People, eager for wealth and power, have searched the ends of the earth to find gold. For thousands of years, people have dug, lied, stolen, and even killed for gold. Governments and individuals have zealously acquired and guarded supplies of gold, but there is never enough.

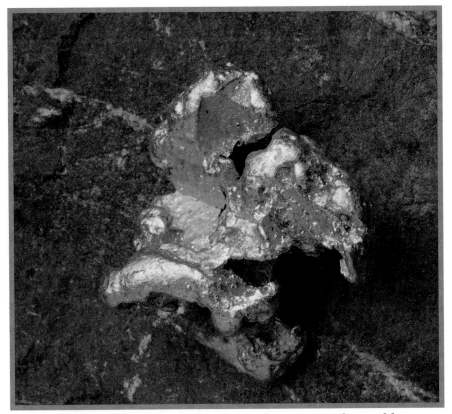

Gold is one of the most valued substances in the world.
This gold nugget was mined in Alaska.

Gold collects in long fractures deep in the rock that makes up the earth's crust. These long veins of gold, called lodes, can remain underground for millions of years. Occasionally, the earth's crust gradually buckles and cracks, and rocks with veins of gold jut to the surface. Over centuries, wind, sun, ice, rain, rivers, and streams erode the rock, exposing the gold. Because gold is very heavy, it settles in valley streambeds, an undiscovered promise of wealth and power, like a secret waiting to be told. This process takes millions of years and has happened in only a few places on earth. The Klondike, a region in the Yukon Territory of Canada near the border of Alaska, is one of these places.

GOLD IN THE NORTH

In 1849, the same year as the California gold rush, a Russian engineer found gold in Alaska. Few people paid attention because the fur trade was considered more important. However, when miners could no longer find gold in California, they drifted north toward rumors of gold in Canada and Alaska. Year after year, a little gold was found—a bit in Juneau, a bit in the Yukon, some in central Alaska—enough to keep hopes rich, but miners poor. About a thousand men roamed the remote river valleys of the Far North looking for the "big strike."

For years, they worked the hills and streams that fed the Yukon River, including the Klondike River and its feeder streams. North

American Indians called the Klondike River the *Thron-duick*, meaning "hammer-water," because they were able to hammer nets into the shallow, shady bottom to catch salmon. But the Klondike River drainage held far more than salmon—it held the answer to prayers, hopes, and dreams. It held the promise of freedom, romance, and adventure.

In the early 1890s, the entire world suffered a terrible economic collapse. Banks closed; railroads and businesses failed. People lost their jobs and many began to hoard gold coins. Times were hard, and fear hardened people's hearts and crushed hopes for the future. Good times seemed gone forever. But people didn't know about the secret in the Klondike creeks—not yet.

TWO

ON THE KLONDIKE CREEKS

In the summer of 1896, George Washington Carmack, a California native living in the Klondike, dreamed about two big salmon with gold-nugget scales and gold-coin eyes. He believed in dreams, and thought this one meant he would have good luck fishing. He was not a miner, and didn't think about the gold-nugget scales and gold-coin eyes. Along with his Indian wife, Kate, and her brothers Skookum (Strong) Jim and Tagish Charlie, he set out to fish.

One of the miners working in the Klondike area, Robert Henderson, had been finding an encouraging bit of "color," or

Geo. Camack

George Washington Carmack

gold, in his pan. While heading back up the Yukon River after resupplying at Fortymile, a Yukon trading post, he met Carmack and his Indian companions. According to miner custom, Henderson told Carmack about his find and invited him to come prospecting, but he added that he didn't want Carmack's Indian friends mining near him.

DISCOVERY

Henderson's attitude angered Carmack and his Indian companions, but about two weeks later, on August 17, 1896, Carmack and his brothers-in-law visited Henderson's camp. They panned for gold now and then along the way, finding little.

Henderson wasn't finding much gold either. When the three men asked to buy tobacco from Henderson, he refused to sell anything to Skookum Jim and Tagish Charlie because they were Indians. Carmack and his brothers-in-law angrily left.

On Rabbit Creek, just over the hill, Carmack, Skookum Jim, and Tagish Charlie stopped to camp and cook some moose meat. As Skookum Jim began washing a frying pan in the creek, he and Carmack spotted a thumbnail-sized gold nugget just lying in the water. After cheering and dancing, the three men dug a few pans of the creek bank and found gold "layered in the rocks like a cheese sandwich," as Carmack later said. They each staked claims along 500 feet (152 m) of the creek bank by carving their names in wooden stakes and pounding them into the ground. Then, while Skookum Jim stood guard, Carmack and Tagish Charlie went to Fortymile to legally file their claims.

Everyone in Fortymile knew Carmack liked to tell exaggerated stories. In Bill McPhee's bar, Carmack bragged about his find to a crowd of miners and told them where to go to stake claims. No one moved. Was this the big strike they had dreamed about or just one of Carmack's stories? But then he showed them a spent shotgun cartridge full of gold. The miners knew instantly from the shape,

Carmack's original claim, named Discovery Claim, on Bonanza Creek

color, and impurities of the gold that it was not from any claims discovered previously. Everyone, including the bartender, rushed out the door to get claims next to George, Jim, and Charlie's.

The one person whom Carmack did not tell about the great find was Robert Henderson, his racist neighbor on the creeks. By the time Henderson found out, the good claims were gone. His unkind heart cost him a fortune.

THREE

A Ton of Gold

During the winter of 1896–97, the miners worked the frozen mud, sand, and dirt along the banks of Rabbit Creek, now renamed Bonanza, and the adjoining Eldorado Creek. Soon everyone from Fortymile and central Alaska had heard about the strike and came to stake claims. A town, Dawson City, quickly grew on the confluence of the Klondike and Yukon rivers. Food supplies dwindled fast as people crowded into the area that winter. With almost no food available to buy, even the millionaires went hungry.

But news of the gold didn't travel very far. The severe winter weather made communication with areas outside the

Klondike and its immediate surroundings almost impossible. All the miners that winter came from within a few hundred miles. The rest of the world would have to wait until spring to find out about the Klondike secret.

That winter was difficult, as most Yukon winters are. Some prospectors (people looking for gold) sold or traded away their claims before knowing if their frozen ground contained gold. There wasn't much to eat beyond whiskey and beans. One starving miner traded his claim for a sack of flour and a side of bacon. Later it produced more than a million dollars in gold.

Finally spring came, and the rivers broke free of ice. Two ships arrived to bring food and supplies and to take passengers back to the United States (Alaska did not become a state until 62 years later). The miners piled gold into the holds of the *Excelsior*, heading for San Francisco, and the *Portland*, heading for Seattle.

GOLD! GOLD! GOLD! GOLD!

On July 15, 1897, eleven months after Carmack pulled the first gold nugget out of Bonanza Creek, the *Excelsior* and its cargo of gold sailed into San Francisco. Newspapers ran stories about the gold brought off the ship and reported that in two days the *Portland* would sail into Seattle with more.

Hard times in Seattle had left many without jobs. Some had little to eat besides the fish they caught. The city couldn't afford fire hoses, and in 1889 the downtown area had caught fire

On July 17, 1897, the Seattle Post-Intelligencer *ran this story announcing the arrival of the steamship* Portland *carrying gold discovered in the Klondike.*

and burned. With no money to rebuild, more jobs had disappeared. It was a downward spiral that seemed to have caught nearly everyone. The gray skies of Seattle reflected the mood and hopes of the whole town.

Then word came about the *Portland*. A reporter met the ship before it sailed into Seattle and filed his story by wire. Huge headlines announced "GOLD! GOLD! GOLD! GOLD!" Five thousand people ran down to the dock to meet the *Portland* as it sailed into Elliott Bay. They watched 68 ragged miners come off the ship with bags, boxes, jars, and even blankets full of gold. They carried more than two tons of gold off the ship.

The news pulsated quickly around the world by telegraph wire: A great gold strike in the Klondike! Gold nuggets as big as eggs! Getting rich was as easy as gathering eggs in a henhouse! Four hours after the *Portland* landed, people were running through the streets of Seattle asking "Are you going?" By the end of the day, over 2,000 people in faraway New York had tried to buy tickets to the Klondike. Around the world, people were packing up and walking out of their old lives. They were all going to be rich. They were all going to find their own ton of gold.

Magazines sent reporters and photographers to cover the story for those who couldn't go. Some who couldn't go themselves "grubstaked" others, paying for their equipment, supplies, and journey in exchange for part of the gold they would surely find. Families pooled their money and voted on one member to go. Coworkers chose people to quit, head north, and bring back gold for everyone.

Soon after the news of gold reached the United States, thousands of hopeful gold-seekers crowded onto ships headed north. Here, the Excelsior, *which had brought the first Klondike gold to the United States a few weeks earlier, leaves San Francisco for Alaska with hundreds of prospectors on board.*

THE GREAT STAMPEDE

By the tens of thousands, people headed north. People from over fifty countries came with dreams of gold, but with very little real knowledge about the difficulties that lay ahead. Many didn't even know that the Klondike was in Canada, and they didn't care. Most knew little about cold and wilderness and less about mining. They were farmers and doctors, shopkeepers and dockworkers, teachers and police officers, carpenters and firefighters, con artists and fishermen. Even the mayor of Seattle joined the rush.

Merchants in Vancouver, Seattle, and San Francisco all saw opportunity in "the great stampede" north. The Canadian police force, called Mounties because they traveled on horseback, required each person entering northern Canada to bring a year's provisions and warm clothing. The equipment required by the Mounties, called a miner's outfit, cost from $250 to $500 in Seattle. In the first year of the rush, Seattle merchants made more money outfitting the stampeders than the value of all the gold mined in the Klondike that year. The depression had ended. Suddenly, there was work for everyone.

Anything with Klondike printed on it seemed to sell, needed or not. Con men worked alongside legitimate merchants. They sold boxed tents, complete with beds and a "lighter than air" stove;

Seattle merchants made huge sums of money outfitting stampeders heading north. Here, a merchant displays a team of sled dogs in a Seattle street. In many cases, the dogs were stolen pets, untrained and ill-suited to the harsh conditions of the Far North.

This sketch from the August 22, 1897, "Klondike Edition" of the New York Journal *shows a stampeder outfitted for the severe Yukon winter—and indicates how much each item will cost.*

gophers trained to dig underground for gold nuggets; sacks of powdered eggs that were really corn flour; and "well-trained" sled dogs that only hours before might have been someone's pet.

The price of a boat ticket north and rates for shipping goods and animals increased ten-fold overnight. The demand for boats far exceeded the number of ships available. Ships from all over the West Coast, regardless of their condition, were pressed into service. Everything from luxury liners to coal barges sailed north, dangerously overloaded with miners, their provisions, and animals. More ships sailed in from Asia. People could not get north fast enough.

There were many routes to the Yukon. Some ships leaving from the northwest coast of the United States or southeastern Canada sailed through the Aleutian Islands to Norton Sound on Alaska's west coast. From there, prospectors could take riverboats 1,600 miles (2,575 km) up the Yukon River to the Klondike. Although this trip bypassed the difficult mountain passes that lay in the path of most other routes, the $1,000 fare was far too expensive for the average prospector. About 90 percent of the people heading to the Klondike sailed from the northwest coast of the United States to the towns of Skagway and Dyea in southeastern Alaska. Ships

Some prospectors leaving from cities in the northwestern United States and southeastern Canada sailed past Unalaska Island to Norton Sound. From there, riverboats carried the miners 1,600 miles (2,575 km) up the Yukon River to Dawson City. Most stampeders, however, couldn't afford the $1,000 fare for this trip. These gold-seekers sailed through the Inside Passage to Skagway or Dyea in southeastern Alaska. From there, the miners hiked treacherous trails to Lake Bennett and then rafted down the Yukon River to Dawson City.

traveling this route passed through the Inside Passage, a protected waterway stretching more than 1,000 miles (1,600 km) from Seattle to Skagway. Once in Skagway or Dyea, the trip to the Klondike had just begun. The prospectors had to prepare for the brutal hike north.

Meanwhile, as the Great Stampede began, the miners already in the Klondike kept working the creeks. It was tough, backbreaking work, but it paid well. Almost every pan brought gold; almost every day brought a new fortune. Before the strike, ten cents worth of gold dust in a pan was considered lucky. Now people frequently got several dollars worth in a pan. Some even found several ounces of gold at one time, worth $57, $83, $212, and an all-time record of $800— over 3 pounds (1.3 kg) of gold in a single pan of dirt!

While stampeders prepared for the long journey north, northern miners already in the Klondike worked the banks of Bonanza and other creeks nearby. These prospectors are mining Skookum Jim's claim.

FOUR

ON THE TRAIL NORTH

Every day more ships pulled into Dyea and Skagway, each loaded with more people, more animals, and more goods. The muddy streets of Skagway were stacked high with supplies and filled with the noise of barter, celebration, and arguments. Almost overnight Skagway went from a small village to an energetic city struck with gold fever.

The price of goods in Skagway and Dyea skyrocketed. Many merchants made far more money selling items in the northern towns than most people did mining gold. One man brought a large stock of bananas up from Seattle to sell for a quarter apiece in Skagway, but they froze on the ship deck and turned to black mush. Just before he threw them away, someone offered him a dollar. That was better than a complete loss, so he handed the man the stock of bananas. The man took one banana and handed the rest back. Within minutes, each black banana had sold for a dollar.

Another man had a pair of old, sickly horses that he sold to new miners. When they discovered their new horses were worthless for packing, the man bought them back at half what they paid him. He then resold them to other miners new in town.

These stampeders have recently arrived in Dyea with their outfits. The toughest part of their journey—the hike to Lake Bennett—still lies ahead.

Jefferson "Soapy" Smith in his saloon

In 1897, Skagway went wild; "Helltown of the North" some called it. Jefferson "Soapy" Smith, con man and gangster, ruled the town—and anyone fresh off the boat was ready game. He ran dishonest businesses, gambling halls, and thief rings. A favorite con of Smith's was his telegraph operation. People new to town frequently came to wire home that they had arrived safely. The next day they would receive an answer that asked them to wire money home immediately. Few noticed that Soapy Smith's telegraph wires weren't connected to anything.

Shops, hotels, and saloons lined the bustling streets of Skagway.

On July 8, 1898, the townspeople of Skagway, tired of being terrorized, met to decide what to do about Soapy Smith. After the meeting started, Smith showed up, gun in hand. Frank Reid, guarding the door, shot Smith in the heart. He died almost instantly, but not before shooting Reid in the pelvis. Reid died eight painful days later. The last Wild-West outlaw was gone. The streets of Skagway became safer, but no quieter or calmer as the boats continued to arrive.

During the winter of 1897–98, the first of the Great Stampede, more than 70 feet (21 m) of snow fell over the mountain passes. Illness, filth, and discouragement swept through the camps along the trails. What started out as a great adventure quickly turned to misery and even death. Many people never made it north of Skagway. Some, victims of crime or accidents, lost their outfits and turned back. Some stayed to open businesses in Skagway or the tent cities along the trails. Everyone had something to sell and something to buy: packing services, the last hot bath for months, floor space in a bedroom, mining gear, week-old newspapers from the States, food, laundry, horses, liquor, or love.

Most of those who decided to continue north chose to hike the Chilkoot Trail, which began in Dyea, or the White Pass Trail, which began in Skagway. Both trails ended at Lake Bennett, the headwaters of the Yukon River. From the lake, they planned to build riverboats and float 500 miles (800 km) down the Yukon River to the Klondike goldfields.

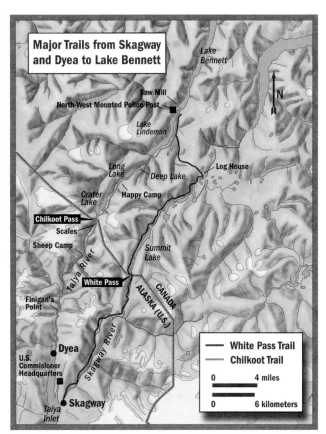

Major Trails from Skagway and Dyea to Lake Bennett

Lake Bennett
Saw Mill
North-West Mounted Police Post
Lake Lindeman
Log House
Long Lake
Deep Lake
Crater Lake
Happy Camp
Chilkoot Pass
Scales
Sheep Camp
Summit Lake
Taiya River
White Pass
ALASKA (U.S.)
CANADA
Finigan's Point
Dyea
U.S. Commisioner Headquarters
Skagway River
Skagway
Taiya Inlet

N

White Pass Trail
Chilkoot Trail
0   4 miles
0   6 kilometers

CHILKOOT TRAIL

The Chilkoot Trail, at 33 miles (53 km), was the shorter of the two trails, but it was also steeper. The trail was so difficult the stampeders called it "33 miles of misery." It began in Dyea and wound upward through a dense mountain forest. Because the trail was too steep for packhorses, the miners usually carried their supplies on their backs, although some hired others to help carry their loads. An basic outfit weighed about 2,000 pounds (907 kg) and couldn't be carried all at once, so the miners divided it into many smaller bundles, each weighing 50 to 100 pounds (23 to 46 kg). They carried a bundle strapped on

The Chilkoot Trail was a treacherous hike. This obstacle lay near Sheep Camp, about halfway up the trail.

Prospectors camp at the base of the Golden Stairs. In the background, a solid line of stampeders climb the Golden Stairs to the summit of Chilkoot Pass.

their back a few miles down the trail, stashed it there, and went back for the next bundle. Moving an outfit this way could take up to forty trips.

Near the top of the pass, they reached a relatively flat area called the Scales. At the Scales, the discouraged hikers caught sight of the steepest part of the trail—the Golden Stairs. In the ice and snow on the face of the steep slope, workers had carved 1,500 steps leading to the summit of Chilkoot Pass, which peaked at 3,550 feet (1,082 m) above sea level. One foot above

At the summit of Chilkoot Pass, the stampeders stowed their supplies and slid back down the pass to fetch another portion of their outfits.

the other, fifteen hundred times, the weary prospectors climbed. One trip up the Golden Stairs was like climbing the Statue of Liberty four times. Some, so disheartened at the sight, sold their outfit for ten cents on the dollar and bought a ticket back home.

Others mentally weighed their load and threw away everything they could do without. Carrying loads weighing 50 to 100 pounds (23 to 46 kg), the hikers climbed through wind and rain, over ice and snow. An unbroken line of humanity headed up the stairs toward a dream of gold. If a stampeder stepped off the trail to rest or adjust his pack for a moment, hours might pass before someone would let him back in line, so intent was everyone on getting to the goldfields.

At the top of the pass, the climbers stored their goods, slid back down to the bottom, and started over again with another heavy bundle. Because the Golden Stairs were so arduous, most people couldn't make more than one trip a day. It took from 20 to 40 days to carry the average outfit over the pass. Some hired Chilkoot Indians as packers. The Indians, known for their strength, charged $5–$15 for a 100-pound (46-kg) load. Many Indians made far more money than the miners they helped.

On April 3, 1898, a beautiful spring day, the Chilkoot Indian packers refused to climb the trail, insisting that it wasn't safe. Most miners wanted to take advantage of the fine day and kept packing their goods up the Golden Stairs. Soon, the soft, melting snow gave way, and an avalanche roared down the mountains and raced into the pass. Up to 35 feet (10.7 m) of snow buried parts of the trail, killing 64 people and their animals at Chilkoot Pass.

Jack London, a famous writer, crossed the Chilkoot carrying a pack of precious books and writing materials. E. A. Hegg, a photographer, crossed with photography equipment, including hundreds of heavy plate-glass negatives, and goats to pull his sled. Hegg took many of the best photographs of the gold rush, including many in this book.

Others brought over unassembled boats and pre-cut lumber. Someone carried an unassembled piano; another, a crate of chickens. Whatever people thought they needed or could sell for a profit went over the pass on their backs.

WHITE PASS TRAIL

The White Pass Trail was neither as high nor steep as the Chilkoot Trail, but it was about 12 miles (19 km) longer. Because it climbed more gradually than the Chilkoot Trail, it was advertised as an easy route for horses carrying mining outfits. In reality, it was a torturous trail full of giant boulders, sharp rocks, fallen trees, and sheer cliffs. The average packhorse lived only six weeks there, and the trail was eventually littered with horse carcasses. In summer, the trail turned swampy, grew thick with clouds of biting flies, and stank of dead, rotting horses. All winter, storms blew down the trail, bringing cold and misery. During the winter of 1897–98, more than 3,000 horses died on the White Pass Trail. It became known as the Dead Horse Trail.

White Pass Trail, photographed 0.5 miles (0.8 km) south of the summit of White Pass

At Chilkoot Pass and White Pass, each trail crossed from the United States into Canada. At the beginning of the rush, the Canadian Mounties set up a border stop and machine gun at the top of both passes. The Mounties, the true heroes of the Klondike Gold

Frequent snowstorms blew down the White Pass Trail throughout the long winter, making travel difficult and dangerous.

The stench of dead horses made conditions on the White Pass Trail even more unbearable. It eventually became known as the Dead Horse Trail.

A tram, seen operating at the right, was built to tow supplies up Chilkoot Pass. Unfortunately, few stampeders could afford to use it.

Rush, stayed on the frozen mountain crests in the harshest weather and checked everyone's supply of food and warm clothing. They turned back the unprepared, saving many who might have frozen or starved to death.

Eventually, a tram was built to carry goods over Chilkoot Pass, and a railroad was built along the White Pass Trail from Skagway to the town of Whitehorse on the Yukon River. The tram proved too expensive for all but the heaviest objects. The railway was finished in 1900—too late for most of the stampeders going to the Klondike. However, many who spent months hiking to the Klondike from Skagway took the train back from Whitehorse in only two days.

DOWN THE YUKON RIVER

Once the miners reached the frozen Lake Bennett, they set up camp and built a boat or raft. Most found this more difficult than getting across the pass. Few had adequate carpentry skills. First they had to cut trees and haul them to the lake. This required

Once the stampeders reached Lake Bennett, they set about building boats and rafts for the trip down the Yukon River.

long hikes because the nearby hills had already been cut bare for lumber and firewood. Then they had to whipsaw the trees into boards, steam the boards into shape, build the boat, and then fill and seal the boards to make the boat seaworthy. The Mounties taught many miners how to do the job properly and inspected and registered each of the 7,124 boats and rafts.

When the miners finished their boats, they had little to do but wait for the frozen lake to melt. While they waited, they built a log church on the hill overlooking Lake Bennett. Before the

Once on the Yukon River, the stampeders had to negotiate the White-horse Rapids. Many boats capsized, and several miners drowned.

church could be finished, on May 29, 1898, the ice finally broke free and everyone took off for the Yukon.

A few boats immediately sank. Others capsized along the way, losing many precious outfits. Ten people drowned, mostly at Miles Canyon and Whitehorse Rapids (named Whitehorse because the white water looked like the manes of wild, white horses running in the wind). Once past these two rapids, the Yukon River remained relatively calm all the way to Dawson City in the heart of the Klondike. Most people thought the worst was behind and nothing but riches lay ahead. They couldn't have been more wrong.

FIVE

IN THE GOLDFIELDS

Only a year before, the Yukon had been still and empty—quiet in the frozen winter, peaceful in the lush summer. Now it was the center of chaos. Each day, large sternwheeler steamships, riverboats, tugs, and all kinds of small boats arrived at Dawson City and unloaded supplies and hundreds of new miners. After months of hardships, they had finally arrived in the land of riches. They poured into the valleys of the Klondike, but they found no egg-sized nuggets lying around. Getting rich was not going to be as easy as walking through the henhouse.

As the stampeders finally reached the Klondike, boats of all sizes congested the waterfront of Dawson City.

The old-timers in the Klondike, called sourdoughs, had already staked every bit of good creek bank. Nothing was left for the newcomers, called Cheechakos. They could work in the mines as hired hands or travel on to unknown, distant rivers hoping to find another Bonanza. Or, if they had money, they could buy a claim. Some never looked for gold at all. Just reaching the Klondike seemed like a grand achievement and adventure enough.

The stampeders who worked the mines quickly discovered that gold mining in the Far North was difficult, dirty work. Much of the gold was found near bedrock, 20 to 200 feet (6 to 60 m) under the permanently frozen ground. The miners dug deep shafts into the ground by building a bonfire. As it burned, the ground beneath slowly melted and the fire gradually sank. Each day the miners gained another foot of depth.

Once they dug the shaft and supported it with split log walls, they built side tunnels where the dirt looked promising. They chipped away the frozen ground or melted it with fires. The miners working underground filled buckets with dirt and mud. Others hauled the buckets to the surface and dumped them onto big piles. In the spring, when the creek thawed, these piles were washed, shovelful by shovelful, in pans, sluice boxes, and rockers to sift out the gold.

The sluice boxes and rockers separated out the rocks and slowly washed the dirt and gravel down a slanted trough. The

By the time the stampeders arrived on the goldfields, they found, to their great disappointment, that local miners had already claimed all of the gold-rich creek banks. Pictured here is Bonanza Creek, with numerous claims (including Discovery Claim) lining the creek banks.

These miners dig for gold in an underground shaft.

heavy gold was caught in a series of ribs, called riffles, on the trough bottom. Periodically, the miners stopped to clean the gold nuggets, flakes, and dust from the riffles. Then, they shoveled in more dirt and poured in more water, with new enthusiasm or disappointment, depending upon their take.

After digging up piles of dirt, miners "wash out" the gold with an elaborate system of slanted troughs. As the water washes over the dirt in the troughs, most of the material is carried away. The gold, because it is heavier, separates from the dirt and collects in ridges, called riffles, on the bottom of the troughs. Periodically, the miners stopped to clean the gold out of the riffles.

DAWSON CITY

During the summers in the Far North, the sun never sets. In the 24-hour daylight, the mining never stopped, and in Dawson City, the partying never stopped. At the peak of the gold rush, 40,000 people lived in Dawson City, making it one of the largest cities in Canada. After news of gold exploded around the world, 250 steamships sailed the Yukon River, bringing most anything people could want: fresh fruit, fresh oysters, Paris fashions, Chinese silk, the best cigars and whiskey, and even tourists.

Sunday, by law, was a day of rest. Even the mines and Dance Hall Row closed at midnight Saturday. The Mounties kept good

Shops, restaurants, hotels, and entertainment halls catered to the many residents of Dawson City.

Pictured here, the Mounties of Dawson City maintained order and won respect without stifling the celebration in the town.

control without stifling the celebration, and they won everyone's respect. There was not one major gold theft or murder in Dawson.

But Dawson City had its characters. Swiftwater Bill Gates was known for his champagne baths, and for paying a dollar apiece for all the eggs in Dawson so the woman he was arguing with couldn't have her usual egg at breakfast. Big Alex McDonald bought several unproven claims from discouraged miners by promising a small down payment and a larger payment later. He ended up buying some of the most productive mines. One day, he led 100 mules, all loaded with gold, into town. He made over $20 million but quickly spent his fortune, much of it on charities. He died poor in 1909. Klondike Kate and Diamond Tooth Lil, who had a diamond between her front teeth, were favorite dance-hall entertainers. After the rush, Kate Rockwell, with $150,000 in savings, went south and lectured about the Klondike. Lil Lovejoy married a respected lawyer.

Father William Judge, a Jesuit missionary, built a hospital and cared for the ill and dying in the Klondike. Others admired his goodness and claimed to feel better just watching him work. Another great man, surveyor William Ogilvie, was totally fair and incorruptible. Because the miners paced off their 500-foot (152-m) claims—sometimes with very large steps—he carefully remeasured all claims, creating small fraction claims between claims that were too large.

Many of the stampeders kept diaries and told vivid stories of their adventures. One typical miner, a Swedish immigrant named John Nordstrom, was farming poor land when he heard of the strike. The next week he sailed to Skagway with his horses. On White Pass the horses died, someone stole his horse food, and his poorly made boots got soaked and hurt his feet. He returned to Skagway for more horses. There he found

Kate Rockwell, known as Klondike Kate, was a favorite entertainer in Dawson City.

a place to sleep for $2, but the bedroom was crowded with dirty, snoring miners. Instead, he burrowed into a haystack and slept warmly and comfortably. However, he had taken off his boots, and in the morning they were frozen solid and impossible to put on.

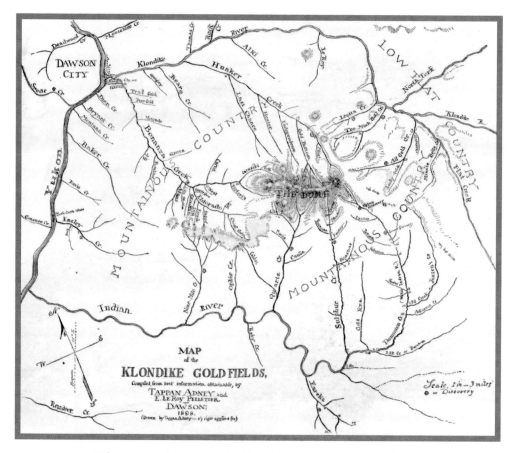

This map, drawn in 1898, shows the many creeks that flow through the Klondike goldfields.

After he and his partners made it to Lake Bennett, they shot and ate their last horse—their first meat in two months. They built their boat easier than most because John had been a lumberjack. In the Klondike they found no gold, no land to claim, and little work. John finally got a job building sluice boxes for $15 a day.

Many months later he met a miner who wanted to sell his claim. John and two friends put up $4,500—and John's dog—to buy it. At the time, no one knew the neighbors on the next claim had hit pay dirt. When John and his partners were dragged into court to fight charges of claim jumping (throwing away someone's markers and claiming that land as your own), the neighbors offered to help if John agreed to sell them his mine. One of the neighbors was related to the judge and persuaded him that John's claim was valid.

John's share of the sale was $15,000, a very good price for an unproven mine. John returned to Seattle, had his first real bath in two years, and invested his money in a shoe store making only good-quality shoes. This was the beginning of the nationwide Nordstrom's Department Stores. Later he learned that his neighbors took $2 million in gold from their mine and another $2 million from his. The department store he founded, however, has earned far more money than any of the mines and is still successful today.

SIX

WOMEN IN THE KLONDIKE

Although most of the people coming over the pass were men,
a good many women and a few children came north. Some
wanted to strike it rich in the goldfields. Others wanted to
strike it rich in business, or by marrying a rich gold miner. Some came
for adventure; some came as missionaries. Some were looking for missing husbands or sons; some were journalists covering the story. Occasionally whole families traveled and worked together. Many women who
came north had nothing to lose. They ran away from abusive families
or from places where a woman couldn't earn a living.

In the Klondike, numerous women made more money than
men. Many who didn't seek their fortune in gold became suc-

cessful running restaurants, hotels, laundries, stores, bars, and dance halls. Others earned a living as entertainers. For an energetic and enterprising woman who could handle difficulties, the Klondike was a land of opportunity.

One successful woman was Mrs. Willis. At 45, just before the big rush, she left San Francisco for Alaska to make her fortune and support her disabled husband. She hauled all her own equipment over Chilkoot Pass, including a sewing machine. Bathing and laundry were difficult in the Yukon. People usually washed with an extra gold pan and threw their clothes away when they became too unbearable. In Dawson City, Mrs. Willis ran a laun-

Many enterprising women made fortunes in the Klondike—by either mining gold or running profitable businesses such as this laundry.

dry service. The cost of operating the service was high—at one point she paid $250 for a box of laundry starch—but the profits were even higher. Between laundry and sewing, she also staked a claim worth $300,000.

Mattie Crosby, an African-American woman, was only 16 when she left Chicago for Skagway in 1900. She climbed the Chilkoot Trail and traveled the Yukon River to Dawson City. She ran "the finest bathhouse in Alaska," offering "medicated, mineral vapor, steam, tub, salt, and fresh water baths." After the rush, she wrote articles for a San Diego newspaper about her adventures and the people she met. She continued to write almost until her death at age 88.

Belinda Mulroney came over the Chilkoot to Dawson with $5,000 worth of hot-water bottles and fabric that she quickly sold for $30,000. She built and ran the elegant Fairview Hotel, known for its white linen tablecloths, fine china and crystal, chamber music, expensive bathroom fixtures, and walls as thin as paper-covered canvas (which they were, because there was so little smooth wood in the area). When she arrived in Dawson, she threw her last half-dollar into the Yukon and swore to never use small change again. Later, she was called the richest woman in the Klondike.

After Kate Carmack's husband discovered gold, her life was thrown into turmoil. She traveled with him but hated the confusion of big cities. Compared to her quiet woods, the cities

Belinda Mulroney owned the Fairview Hotel, one of the most elegant establishments in Dawson City.

were like another planet. To find her way back to her hotel room, she slashed marks on the hotel banisters and hallways with her ax. George loved being famous and quickly found his wife a burden. He soon divorced her. Skookum Jim built a cabin for Kate in the Yukon. She was much happier there than in the strange streets of San Francisco, but she always wore a necklace made of gold nuggets she had picked up that first summer on Bonanza Creek.

The few children in Dawson City were adored by homesick miners.

As time passed, more and more women found their way to the gold towns of the north. By 1900, women from the United States and Canada made up 23 percent of Skagway's population and 10 percent of Nome's. Children were far fewer and more precious. Many miners were homesick, and they delighted in seeing a child or patting a baby. They often gave gold nuggets as treats to the children they met.

SEVEN

THE SEARCH FOR GOLD MOVES ON

I wanted the gold, and I sought it;
I scrambled and mucked like a slave.
Was it famine or scurvy—I fought it;
I hurled my youth into a grave.
I wanted the gold, and I got it—
Came out with a fortune last fall,—
Yet somehow life's not what I thought it,
And somehow the gold isn't all.

—Robert Service *Spell of the Yukon*

Today, modern machinery mines the banks of Bonanza Creek.
This machinery can collect gold missed by the more primitive
equipment of the gold rush days.

As miners spread across the north, every year or two brought
a new strike in another place. In 1898, "Three Lucky Swedes"
found gold on the Arctic shoreline, and everyone rushed to mine
gold from the sand beaches of Nome. In 1902, Felix Pedro discovered gold near Fairbanks. Several other strikes across central
Alaska followed. In the twenty years after George Carmack first told
the boys in McPhee's bar about his gold, more than 339 tons of
gold were taken out of the Klondike and other areas of the north.
The best year was 1900, when miners took out 45 tons of gold—
worth $22 million then and about $600 million now.

Gold mining continues today. When the price of gold rose,
large companies with sophisticated machinery began remining
the hills and valleys of the north. They sifted through the tailing

piles—dirt left behind by previous miners—looking for gold missed by the stampeders. A few individuals still work the creeks, but now they use generators, hydraulic hoses, backhoes, and bull-dozers. Each summer, tourists and amateur miners come to the beaches of Nome to try their luck. Gold is there, but it is fine gold dust. The days of the easy, big payloads are gone.

THE KLONDIKE 100 YEARS LATER

Evidence of the great 1898 adventure still lingers along the Klondike Trail. Skagway and Dawson City maintain much of their gold rush flavor, but it is for their new bonanza—the tourist trade. On the Yukon River, ghostly skeletons of the great white sternwheelers remain tied to the shore. The White Pass Railroad still runs along the narrow mountain cliffs, using the original cars with potbelly

Modern Skagway maintains the spirit of the
gold rush and is a popular tourist attraction.

Just outside of Dawson City, the remains of great sternwheelers on the Yukon River serve as a constant reminder of the gold rush.

stoves in one corner. But the passengers are tourists, not dirty miners and fancy dance-hall girls.

Outside of Dyea on the Chilkoot Trail, the old tram's steam engine sits in the undergrowth, its cable twisting along the ground. At the Scales, rotting blankets, worn shoes, rusting food tins, and metal of all kinds mark the remains of discarded dreams. Decaying tent platforms, shredded canvas, rusting mattress springs, and broken bottles lie where the old camps stood. The hills around Lake Bennett are thick with forests, as if gold madness had never cut them bare.

This mass movement of people permanently tied the northern wilderness to the rest of the world. It hasn't stood empty and apart since. The Klondike Trail from Seattle to Dawson City is now an International Historical Park. Visitors from around the world come to walk in the dreams of the old stampeders. Each year, more than a million people visit exhibits in Seattle, Skagway, and Dawson City. Each summer, about 3,500 people once again follow the promise of adventure and climb the Chilkoot Pass.

In 1897, everyone dreamed of leaving their homes for

Klondike riches. Of the 100,000 people who actually did, only 40,000 made it all the way to the Klondike. Of those, only about 5,000 found any gold at all, and only 300 found $10,000 or more, enough to be rich. Of those lucky 300, just 50 kept their fortune more than a few years.

One of those fifty was George Carmack. Before he found gold, he never cared much about money. But he enjoyed his fortune and increased it with some profitable investments. He died, still a rich man, in Vancouver, Canada, in 1922.

Some prospectors, whether or not they found gold, were broken by the experience, dying penniless and lonely. Most stampeders, however, discovered secrets as valuable as gold. The hardships and camaraderie along the trail strengthened them, and they returned home better, if not richer, people. All who came north took risks to change their lives. They left with rich tales of their adventures in those golden days on the Klondike.

Each year, thousands of hikers retrace the steps of the stampeders on the Chilkoot Trail. Even in summer, snowfields cover parts of the trail.

FOR FURTHER READING

NONFICTION

Adney, Tappan. *The Klondike Stampede of 1897–98*. Vancouver: Whitecap Books, 1995.

Becker, Ethel Anderson. *Klondike '98: E. A. Hegg's Gold Rush Album*. Portland, OR: Binfords and Mort, 1972.

Cooper, Michael L. *Klondike Fever: The Famous Gold Rush of 1898*. New York: Clarion Books, 1989.

Dawson City. Anchorage: Alaska Geographic Society, 1988.

Murphy, Claire Rodulf, and Jane Haigh. *Gold Rush Women*. Seattle: Alaska Northwest Books, 1997.

Ray, Delia. *Gold! The Klondike Adventure*. New York: Lodestar Books, 1989.

POETRY AND FICTION

London, Jack. *Call of the Wild*. Norman: University of Oklahoma Press, 1995.

—*Jack London's Stories of the North*. New York: Scholastic, 1989.

—*White Fang*. New York: Puffin Books, 1985.

Service, Robert. *Collected Poems of Robert Service*. New York: Putnam, 1989.

INTERNET RESOURCES

Ghosts of the Gold Rush

http://www.gold-rush.org/

This site offers lots of historical information about the gold rush complete with stories and photos from the Klondike.

Gold Rush Centennial Photographs, 1893–1916

http://www.educ.state.ak.us/lam/library/hist/goldrush/table.html

An exhibition of photographs of the gold rush from the Alaska State Library

Golden Dreams: The Quest for the Klondike

http://www.wshs.org/text/klondike/index.htm

This is an online historical and photographic exhibition by the Washington State Historical Society. You'll find many gold rush photographs here.

The History Net

http://www.TheHistoryNet.com/

Check out the American history section of this online source of historical information for a great article on the Klondike stampeders.

Klondike Gold Rush Centennial

http://www.wolfenet.com/~yoame/klon/

This site offers lots of information about the gold rush including stories of life on the trails and profiles of the major gold rush characters.

Klondike Gold Rush National Historical Park
http://www.nps.gov/klgo/
Many regions of the gold rush have been preserved in a national
park. The park has two headquarters—one in Seattle and another
in Skagway. This site offers information about all areas of the park.

Skagway, Alaska
http://www.skagway.org/
http://www.skagway.com/
Skagway, Alaska, retains much of its gold rush flavor. These
sites offer information on travel, lodging, events, activities, and
the history of the town.

White Pass & Yukon Route Railway
http://www.whitepassrailroad.com/
Much of the White Pass railroad has been restored and is open to
tourists. This site offers information about riding on the railway.

INDEX

Page numbers in *italics* indicate illustrations.

ABOUT THE AUTHOR

Donna Walsh Shepherd lives in Alaska with her husband and three sons. She teaches literature and writing at the University of Alaska. Ms. Walsh Shepherd has also written these other First Books: *Uranus, The Aztecs, Tundra,* and *Auroras: Light Shows in the Night Sky,* which was named to the Science Books & Film Best Children's Book List for 1995. Many years ago, she met one of the original stampeders. He was 92, managed a four-story apartment building without an elevator, and easily ran up and down the stairs. She has climbed the Chilkoot Trail and panned for gold, but she has never found even one flake.

SPENCER LOOMIS SCHOOL
1 Hubbard Lane
Hawthorn Woods, IL 60047

DATE DUE

GAYLORD			PRINTED IN U.S.A.